POEMS

FROM

MY

HEART

BY:

Judith A. Knox

Published in 2003 by:

Paramount Printers Ltd.
1207 – 3 Avenue South
Lethbridge, Alberta
Canada
T1J 0J7

Credits:

Title "Poems From My Heart"
by Rebecca Judith-Lynn Prepsl

Cover and photos by:
Tige & Michelle Lou
Calgary, Alberta.

Cover : P.E.I. Lighthouse

Pencil drawing of my dad by:
Dad's first cousin, Charles Pettipas

Canadian Cataloging in Publication Data

Knox, Judith A. 1944 –
Poems From My Heart

jneknox@shaw.ca or P.O. Box 146
Coalhurst, AB, Canada T0L 0V0
1 (403) 329-0718

ISBN 0-9733483-0-5

… I'M DOING WHAT I SHOULD HAVE DONE YEARS AGO, WHICH IS FINDING OUT WHO I AM AND WHAT I WANT. I WANT TO HAVE A CHOICE. AND WHEN I MAKE DECISIONS THROUGH CHOICE, NOT DUTY, IT HAS TO BE BETTER FOR ME AND FOR THE PEOPLE WHO LOVE ME AND THE PEOPLE I LOVE.

- LOUISE FLETCHER

4

ACKNOWLEDGMENTS

****

First and foremost I recognize the one
to whom I owe my very being,
God
for giving me the talent to achieve my goal.

Second, this book would never have become a reality
if it were not for the following people
who encouraged me to attain it.
My faithful husband Ed,
Dr. Billy & Donna Hover,
Connie & Erkki Laitinen,
and to those who were my inspiration
for these words of rhyme.
And to my dear friend,
Mr. Art Plewes,
for his editing services.
Also, to Dr. B. D. Schaber,
for debugging the final page.
I thank each of you for all of your help.

Last but not least I thank you, the readers,
who purchased this book.
To you I am humbly grateful.

****

INTRODUCTION

Writing this book became a reality after many friends would say, " You write good stuff and you should write a book". My husband told me the same thing many years before, that I should put my poems in a book. But who listens to their husband?

It was after writing a Poem for a Fiftieth Wedding Anniversary for my Dentist and his wife that I made the decision to put my poems in a book. If only for a legacy for my grandchildren and their generations to follow.

So with enough encouragement from my husband and finally finding enough courage within myself I humbly wrote what you see before you today. Whether I write "good stuff" will be decided only by the reader.

With the exception of the Anniversary poems the creation time for each one usually would be approximately anywhere between ten to twenty, or twenty five minutes, give or take a few.

They have been written on toilet paper rolls, Kleenex boxes, backs of pocket books, and cardboard from panty hose packages, I have used the palm of my hand, or anything that would retain the ink or lead from the object I would be holding at the time.

I have to be in the mood before I can pen my thoughts. However the mood can strike at anytime or anyplace. It usually strikes me at a time when I have nothing available to write on or write with. Usually in the middle of the night.

I dare not procrastinate writing my thoughts in rhyme at that time or else it is lost forever. I made that mistake on several occasions and I'm sure they were the ones that would have made my book reach Oprah's Book Club. (The Lord blessed me with a sense of humor)

So, dear reader, what you have before you is the result of one of my goals in life. I am not and do not claim to be a poet. I am just an average person writing average thoughts that come from my heart and a wanting to fulfill one of her dreams. One of my dreams is to publish a book.

It is my intention that the reader will glean from this book, tidbits of humour, hope, encouragement, and a longing to achieve whatever goal in life that you desire.

I humbly thank you for acquiring and reading "Poems From My Heart".

DEDICATION

I dedicate this, my first, book to
my faithful husband , Ed, of over forty years
without
his love, support,
friendship, and forgiveness, I would be as
a
wilted plant
without the life giving supply
of living water.
Thank you my darling
for
having enough love
for the
both of us, as
you had first promised.

TABLE OF CONTENTS

INSPIRATION

ON A PERSONAL NOTE

THE LIGHTER SIDE

TABLE OF CONTENTS (cont)

FRIENDSHIPS

DOWN MEMORY LANE

MEMORIES OF MY DAD

MISCELLANEOUS

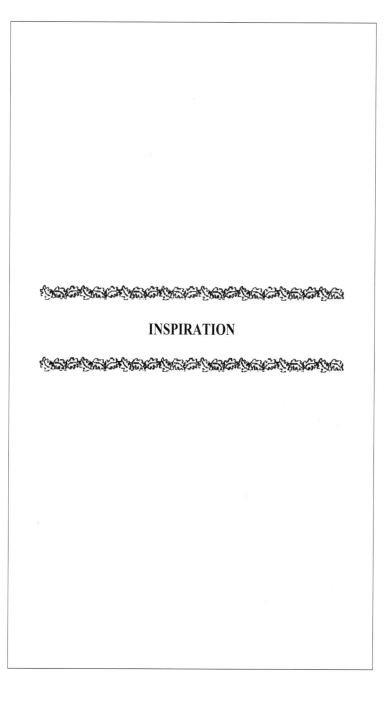

INSPIRATION

WHEN YOU HARDEN YOUR HEART

When you harden your heart against repentance
you commit the unpardonable sin.
When you give up your soul for prideful ways,
then Satan is already within.

As Judas chose his position
by wanting on Christ's right hand side.
Our hearts, too, are polluted.
Our vanity all puffed out with pride.

Jesus gave us the example.
For these things He suffered and died.
While we contend for a high spot
instead of in prayer do reside.

While pride and supremacy rule us.
Self exaltation rules us too.
Jesus gave us the perfect example.
"You should do as I have done for you."

He, again, will be served and honored
by those who would be ready to partake,
in His glory of seeing souls redeemed.
We must tell them before it is too late.

Tell them the story of one man.
Who, from heaven to earth, came down.
Born in a manger of hay and dirt,
not a palace or under a crown.

The night He was betrayed took boldness,
on the part of the offending man.
He sold Him for plenty of silver.
Then took his life by his own hand.

Jesus' body was battered and broken.
A symbol we find in the bread.
He said to remember Him always
and the reason He ended up dead!

POEM OF HOPE

The day may be bleak with darkness, and the devil to you might say:

" Don't bother about your hope my friend,

follow me and I'll show you a way...

A way to make you rich and famous, a way for you to have many friends,

a way for all of your dreams to come true.

But I want your soul in the end."

It's times like this that you'll need to talk. So get down on your knees and pray.

Say: " Jesus, please give me the hope that

I need to resist the devil's sly ways."

Satan just can't take your soul or your heart. He can't give you all true friends.

Oh he can make you rich and give you the fame.

But the cost is:...your soul...to him.

Jesus asks nothing but to follow Him and the way won't always down slope.

But with Jesus to guide you and His arms

to hide you you'll never again lose all hope.

WHEN JESUS ROLLS YOUR HEADSTONE AWAY

Sleep my friend and rest while there's no worries to plague your day.
Sleep and rest till that great hour. When Jesus rolls your headstone away.

You'll awake refreshed and fully changed. The grave cannot bid you to stay.
No pain will you suffer, no tears will you shed. When Jesus rolls your headstone
away.

What a sight there to greet you when you open your eyes and He spreads out His
arms your way. He'll embrace you and bid you gently to come. When Jesus rolls
your headstone away.

The table is set. Your family will come. And friends who have long passed away,
will meet you and yours at the table all set. When Jesus rolls your headstone away.

I'll be there too. and my family.....I hope. For that's what you and I prayed. That
they would find Jesus and join us right there. When Jesus rolls our headstones
away.

GOOD NEWS

Oh have you heard? Oh have you heard the Good news that's going round?

That Jesus Christ the Son of God is coming to Lethbridge Town!

All the saints whoever lived will rise to be set free.

Won't that be great to see them rise? I'll pray for you please pray for me.

Some of us who have no hope of the Savior Lord to see.

Don't despair it is only Satan trying to discourage thee.

Believe the Lord for He has said " I'll return to set you free."

So get thee behind me Satan cause the arms of the Lord are protecting me!

LIFE IS LIKE A PUZZLE

Life is like a puzzle, every piece should fit in place.
When the final piece is fitted,
is like a runner finishing the race.

All you've done should be completed,
there should be nothing left to do.
You should be ready for The Master
when He finally calls for you.

Because an unfinished puzzle
is like an unfinished life.
It's like an almost kind of wedding
with a husband, but no wife.

We shall pass this way but only,
just once is all we get.
So we better make it count for good,
for those we haven't yet.

The good we do for others
will carry on always.
We may not be here to see it.
But it will live on past our days

So, do something nice for someone
before it is too late.
Remember, life is like a puzzle and
the pieces they may break.

It won't hurt you to be nicer.
To be nicer there's no cost.
Remember life's a puzzle and
your pieces may get lost.

So, please keep it altogether
and make it count for him.
For to lose just one piece of the puzzle
would be like the Unpardonable Sin.

THE MIRROR

I look into the mirror

and what do I see?

A stranger, a sinner

gazing back at me.

The eyes are so heavy.

The gray hair just hangs down.

Oh! What a sight to see.

I, then, turn around.

With my head in my hands,

The tears gently fall.

I cry " Lord forgive me,

I can't win at all."

A hand on my shoulder.

A voice gently speaks.

" My dear, dear, Woman

for what so you seek?"

The tears flow quite swiftly now.

Harsh sobs wretch my soul.

I sob "I'm a sinner Lord

please make me whole."

The voice gently speaks again

saying "Child, Look and see."

I look back into the mirror.

Behold! A brand new me!

GLENBARD CEMETERY

There's a little spot in Nova Scotia, not far from James River Town.

The place is named Glenbard, where my bones will finally lay down.

There's a church that's been there forever, and many services it has held.

A lot of good folks lie beside it not hearing the ringing of the bell.

Someday I, too, will rest there, until my Savior's face I see.

I'll never know what's happening or what the future will be.

That little spot is quite tranquil except for the cars passing by.

The moon and stars still shine down at night on the good folks, beneath them lie.

My remains may come from another place, a home that I call "The West".

But when my day of departure falls, Glenbard will be "My Rest".

I'D RATHER

I'd rather fall asleep in the grave
then to make my bed in Hell.
I'd rather never bear the wrath of God.
I'd rather climb a mountain
than fall on bended knee
to worship Satan and his very evil squad.

I'd rather drink form the fountain
than choke on the burning Lake.
I'd rather buffet the swelling of the seas.
I'd rather be whipped and beaten
than to deny my precious Lord.
But maybe so like Peter, so like me.

Help me Jesus. Help me Lord.
Help me overcome and gain the victory.
For I'm so weak and tired and my body is so poor.
But thank You Jesus, thank You, for loving me.

LITTLE CHILDREN

There's nothing like the singing voice
of children gathered round.
A teacher telling stories
of god's love that abounds.

They're small, sweet, and innocent.
They are impressed by what they see.
So we must never hurt a child,
for God suffers them, " Come unto me."

Anyone who'd hurt a child
is one who'd better beware.
Because the wrath of God is strong,
it'd be best if you'd just disappear.

For God so loved the little children
and He suffered them to; "Come unto me."
We, too, should love the little ones
if the dear Lord we want to see.

Yes, we must become as a little child
if the Lord we want to see.
Because He loves the children so
the way He loves you and me.

So don't despair, the Lord's near you
and wants to lead you home.
But Satan is always near us too
to tell us when we're wrong.

So when he comes and tempts you,
get on your knees and pray.
Ask the Savior to send His Son,
to escort you throughout the day.

TAKE HEART

I wish I knew a time and place
when we look at God face to face
and say we're hurting and oh, how sad
we take the good but not the bad.
Why must it be like this on earth?
You lead a life with all the hurts.
I guess, I suppose if all was grand
we'd never think to take God's hand,
and trust in Him no matter what,
because His love is all we've got
that keeps Satan and his at bay
so they can't rip our souls away.
Yes, living this Hell on earth is true
oh how our hearts get torn in two
and when we think there is no more
death comes in from another door.
But God has not promised skies always blue
or tears will be taken from me or you,
except in heaven that day we'll see
the promise fulfilled for you and for me.
Take heart and weep to cleanse your soul
while time dulls the pain on its forward roll.
There is a blessing to be found.
We seem to stand taller when we are low down.
So God go with you and go also with me,
until we're united for eternity.

EVERYBODY NEEDS SOMEBODY

Have you ever felt down and out while praying on bended knee?
Could you not hear the Lord tell you " Leave your sinful ways and follow me?"

Are you not troubled and in despair because you felt so low?
Well don't despair your Friend is here and He does love you so.

You may feel unworthy when someone tells you it's so.
But remember Jesus paid the price so He won't let you go.

Everybody needs somebody to tell them they are loved.
I have Jesus and so can you. Just look to the heaven above.

Just read the good book and you will find within its treasured pages.
A love letter full of promises that sustained people through the ages.

Do not let the devil tempt you into thinking you are lost.
For God knows you were worth every drop of blood on the cross.

So no matter how you feel be it happy or be it sad.
Just remember Jesus loves you. He's the best friend you'll ever have.

HELP ME

Father, help me, please come for me now.
I can't make it through this night.
Only You can take what's wrong,
and forever make it right.
Sometimes I'm in this dark hole,
so black that I get scared.
In this confusing world of sin,
I'm afraid I won't be spared.
Satan tells me day after day,
I am his: "A Toy of Play"
I get weak and then give in,
To the hatred You call sin.
The more I fall the lower I go.
Until within a voice I know,
calls softly to me: "Don't give up
come to my table, take my cup.
Don't listen to Satan or what he claims.
I died for you. I know you name.
I died for you, I will forgive
I died for you, that you might live."

THE PASTOR'S SOLES

As I looked at the bottoms of his shoes I saw a story to unfold.

This man of God put many miles on them because of the worn out soles.

Where did he go so many times to make the soles wear thin?

I'd like to think that he enjoyed the walk of doing God's errand for Him.

Those shoes most likely visited the sick, but also the sad and the poor.

They also tread upon dangerous ground and hurried to somebody's door.

Many miles went on those shoes that wore the soles so thin.

But God will reward this faithful man who walked many miles for Him.

So should you see the Pastor praying in church and on his bended knee.

Don't be ashamed by the worn out shoes. They're worn out cause of you and me.

WE CAN'T SEE

We can't see the glory because of the gloom.

We can't see the Coming because of the doom.

We can't see salvation because of our sins.

We can't hear the knocking when our Saviour wants in.

So look to the future with hope but beware.

Don't worry about doom and hopeless despair.

He said " Come to me, I will give you all peace".

So under His wings, till He comes, I will sleep.

THE STORM

The storm came so quickly that I couldn't prepare.
It came swift and painful. I was caught unaware.

I tried to outrun it and yes even hide.
I didn't want to face it cause I thought I would die.

It was one of the many I faced in my time.
But could I conquer it? The decision wasn't mine.

But to fight it is tiring and it drains on my strength.
I can't go it alone because of its length.

There's only one thing that I need to do.
And that's fall on my knees and cry out to You.

Please Lord; fight it with me to conquer this test.
But God said, " I'll take it. I'll do the rest."

So as with the other storms harassing my life.
I left it with Jesus to take care of the strife.

So, whatever storm comes sweeping your way.
Just give it to Jesus. He'll accept it always.

FORGIVE ME LORD

I've fallen short of parenting. I've fallen short in life.

My children do not come to church,

and one has left his wife.

I've failed God by doing things that I ought not to do.

The devil sure has pegged me right,

in my weakness through and through.

I make excuses for my faults, and say God doesn't mind.

But when it comes to helping souls,

For Him I lag behind.

My children hated the Sabbath Day, to them it was a chore.

I tried, wrongly, to make them mind.

But they only hated it more.

Sit up straight! Don't talk back! Don't you dare get wet!

Mind your manners when we're out!

Or else "The Spoon" you'll get!

Instead of loving them to You. I took the devil's way,

screaming, scolding, and spanking them,

and not showing them Your way.

Others I can love to church and wink at all their sins.

But when it comes to my own kids

I'm way too hard on them.

Maybe someone else can try to bring them back to Thee.

But as for my house and myself,

I'm not rightly trusted to be.

So please forgive me precious Lord for the wicked thing I've done.

Driving your children away from You,

instead of leading them home.

I WANT TO GO HOME

I want to go now I can't wait for the day until the Lord calls me home.
I'm tired and lonely and aching and sore.
I want a new body to call my own.

Oh Look! There's David and Samson and there's Esther too.
Excuse me while I call out their names.

I'll ask them to join us for lunch at my place.
And later we'll play some heavenly games.

I hear the angels already starting the choir
and the bells they're getting ready to ping.

It's my turn to join them in heavenly song.
And to think that I couldn't even sing.

NEW OCEANS

You cannot discover new oceans
Without drifting along with the tide.
You cannot discover you potential
Until you discover yourself from inside.

The oceans you travel will guide you
To where your heart longs to be.
But you cannot travel forever
And expect to sail worry free.

Someday you'll wake up discouraged
And discover you can't continue on.
Some days the tides will lift you so high.
Some days you'll awake upside down.

Then others will make it smooth sailing.
When all is well deep within.
You'll know you've accomplished something
When you're beached at a new shore again.

But until you reach you own ocean
And find there what is in store.
You cannot discover NEW oceans
Unless you lose sight of OLD shores.

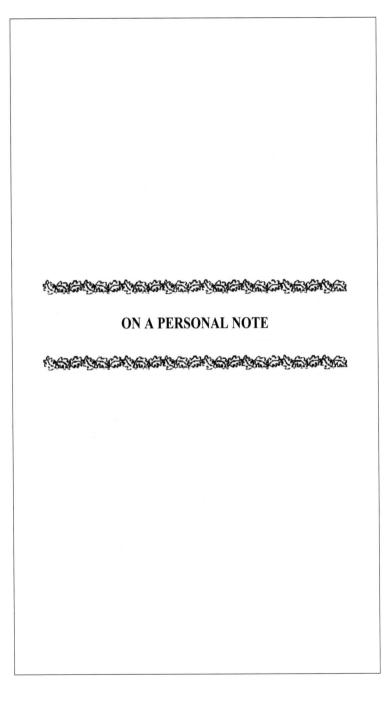

ON A PERSONAL NOTE

ABANDONED

Whatever happened long ago in the year of "43"
when a girl found out about the facts of life
and she was a mother to be?

A single parent she, then, became
on May 4th, of "44".
It wasn't a popular thing to be
so she thought she'd even the score.

She gave the baby age six months old
away to a couple who, when,
took the child and raised it up
the best way they thought of then.

How could she know the child would grow
and shocked she would become,
to find out after 14 years,
that Mary was not her mom?

THE BABE AT MARY'S DOOR

Betty, Betty where can you be
when you left Halifax in " 43"
to bear a child in "44" ?
The babe you left at Mary's door.

She's searching still for the mother who,
gave her up and never knew
to where she went or what's in store
for the innocent babe left at Mary's door.

Did Mary know? Did Mary care
if you or her father had an affair?
Was it love or was it more
for the babe you left at Mary's door?

She's all grown up with babes of her own.
She truly loves them one by one.
She often thought to even the score
with the woman who left her at Mary's door.

She was confused and uttered this oath
for the Angel of Death to outpour.
it's final sleep forever to creep
o'er the babe left at Mary's door.
How could you leave an offspring
without a trace or more?

Did you not know she'd want you back?
the babe left at Mary's door.
How many lies were uttered
to cover up those and more?
To hear the news of a mother who,
left her at Mary's door.

Many years have come and gone
since when her life was poor.
She's now grown into womanhood…..
the babe left at Mary's door.

ODE TO JUDY ANN

Oh why did you give me away that day? Was it my fault you don't care?

I was a babe that knew of no hate.

Mother!...why weren't you there?

Did you ever think of your abandoned child or what had become of me?

Although she was nice and tried her best,

It wasn't the same.. you see.

She only knew how to love but one and that was herself....Although

She brought me up not to lie or steal

And for a while I did love her so.

She killed my love the day she said, to that family I didn't belong.

What do you say to a woman like that

A mother you thought her all along?

I often wondered why you did leave, me for somebody else.

You let me grow up as another's child.

Did you ever feel shame for yourself?

I never knew a real home, one out of love and trust.

The place I knew was full of hate,

mostly from drink and lust.

But as I grew older my love showed through, to those who'd do me no wrong.

I put up a front happiness and smiles,

While crying most nights all along.

The mother I have now is the one I do love. She's faithful, kind, and true.

She shows me her love, which I really need,

In all that she says she will do.

To those who have a mom like mine now, be faithful, be kind and be true.

You'll never know the love that she gives,

Until she's gone forever from you.

So treat her with love the rest of your life, in all that you say and will do.

Your mother may have her many faults.

But one of them isn't you.

THE GIRL

How could you know the hurt would show?

on the girl who is one man's wife?

It never leaves... the hurt still shows. One must continue on with one's life.

Someday the answers may be there

for the girl who cried so long.

For a mother who left so much unsaid to the child she did so wrong.

But, yes, the girl is married now.

To a family she now belongs.

The children love her all they can. But her heart holds an empty song.

It's a song that needs an ending.

Be it happy or be it sad.

There are questions that need answers, for the girl child is no longer mad.

So what will happen to the empty song?

When the final verse is through?

Will you know or will you not of what you have put her through?

FORGIVE ME MOTHER

You took me in as a wee small child. You brought me up your way.

You instilled in me certain values and such

that I still believe in today.

I wasn't always an easy child.... to lead, or guide, or raise.

But you tried to do the best you could

with what you knew those days.

Then the time of Revelation came when I felt abandoned and sore.

So I wrote you then and told you off.

I'd bother you no more.

It was the worst mistake I could have made. Because I was so dumb.

I wounded you so badly then,

now the wound I feel is my own.

Twenty-one years passed by all too quick, and younger we are not.

The empty years without memories of you

is exactly what I've got.

Twenty-one years passed by all too quick, and younger we are not.

The empty years without memories of you

is exactly what I've got.

Oh , I have family and I have my friends of that you will agree.

But you're the one that I've done wrong to

and forgiveness I would like to plea.

Would you forgive me once again of being a spoiled child!

I never should have hurt you so

because pain is never mild.

If you will ease my guilt of shame, I promise to agree.

never again to hurt you so,

with love to you from me.

ROTTEN BANANAS

I'd eat the rotten bananas. The rotten bananas I'd eat.
*Hal White was a mean old man.
He'd sell fruit upon the street.
Yes, he was a street vendor.
At the Fruit Market he had a stall.
My mother worked for him daily,
cleaning and giving her all.

His fruit would come to his house, a flat on Falkland St.
There were oranges, apples, and bananas.
The rotten ones I'd love to eat.

But one night I remember, ah yes I remember it well.
He sat reading the evening paper,
on the news part he'd like to dwell.
I was beneath his knees just laying.
Laying there looking at books.
When he bent over and whispered to me.
"P-s-s-t, look up here…. Look."

I lifted my four year old head up
and saw something fluttering around.
The pipe that he was smoking
was now turned upside down.

I remember screaming loudly,
and crying out for my mom.
I heard her cursing and swearing.
Then came quickly on the run.

I couldn't see for looking. I kept my eyes shut tight.
The pain that I felt burning, lasted long, throughout the night.

Yes, Hal White was a mean old man,
and a fruit vendor on the street.
He was a keeper of good bananas.
But, the rotten ones I loved to eat.

*not his real name

ANNIVERSARY POEM

You loved me in the " 60's"
that June day you kissed my head.
and whispered softly to me
someday we would be wed.

I laughed at you for saying that.
and thought it would never be.
You proved me wrong next date later
when I was "your bride to be."

You found me when I needed you most.
You saved me from an awful fate.
At that time my life was a living hell
But you chose me as your mate.

The following year in February
we both said "Yes, we do."
I found it hard to have a mate.
But I couldn't say that for you.

Our children numbered from one to four.
of them we were so pleased.
Three boys and a girl to complete our love
and add to "The Knox Family Tree"

Edward was the oldest Son.
Brad and Steve came next,.......fast.
Our daughter Shierra would be the one,
Who'd finally be the last.

We made adjustments as time went on.
We worked from dawn to dusk.
It was not a fairy tale marriage.
Making it work was a definite must.

There were a few who could have shared
A dream or two with us.
But when the final curtain fell.
The only two left standing was....Us.

Sometimes we wished to be alone.
To let our thoughts come through.
Sometimes in solitude we'd find,
that no one else would do.

So many years of side to side
together hand in hand.
You loved me and I loved you.
There was no other man.

Ah, yes the years are passing by.
Our youth has gone before.
Our eyes are dim. Our teeth are false.
Our joints are always sore.

But when the last day finally comes,
and we must say good-bye.
Remember , I will be "Your Girl."
And you'll always be, " My Guy."

With a love like this how can we fail
to see what the years have done?
They have nurtured a relationship,
two hearts that bloomed as one.

If I were given a magic wand,
to make some changes new
of all the past married years.
not one would I change with you.

A marriage like ours comes just once.
No matter how long one seeks.
I guess the Good Lord knew us both.
When He granted us destined to meet.

I have shared my best years with you Ed.

Of that I would not end.

You gave to me your best years too.

I thank you, my lover and my friend.

So now I'll say on this special day.

I pray you're as happy as I.

And thank you for past memories

Love "Your Girl" to " My Guy."

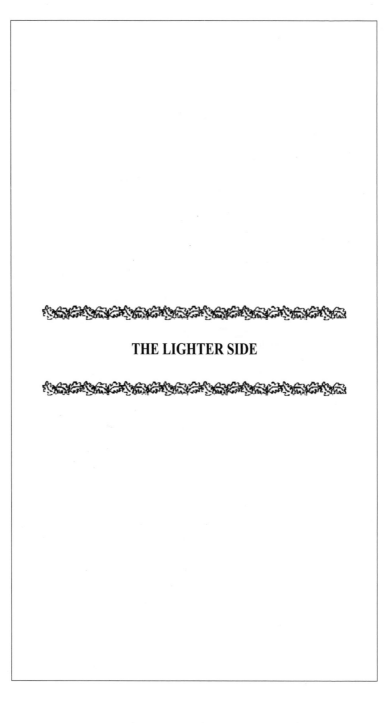

THE LIGHTER SIDE

TAXES

Taxes here and taxes there and only the poor must pay.
The middleman who finally gets must give back they say.
The rich man who makes more than us is sure safe in that bracket.
But, the poor man and the middleman must pay for the rich man's racket.

The poor get poorer and the rich get richer the middle class gets poorer too.
Because of the politics that runs wild a tax scam is not new.
Then it's only a matter of time before you'll make more than me.
I'll know what I'll do. I'll tax you. Then who'll laugh last you'll see.

We'll tax this and we won't tax that.
We'll get you so confused. You'll see.
Then by the time we tax you more,
You'll never make more than me.

POOR GRAMMA

Early in the morning way before dawn
I sit at my desk with the computer screen on.

I view all the messages and click on a few.
I forward out allot of them
Plus the funny ones from you.

I haven't had so much fun since I was just a child.
Sending lots of e-mail would drive my grandma wild.

If she came back from the grave that is....

Can you imagine the look of surprise?
That would greet her and shock her
From her toes to her eyes.

Oh the feminine commercials
Would surely do her in
If she could come back
to see the dumb mess we are in.

There's commercials about undergarments
Bras, panties and such.
Gramma would turn beet red
And make such a fuss.

She'd call us all hussies
She'd slap all the men
she'd need only one minute of South Park
before she'd die all over again.

THE SIMPLE LIFE

Life seemed simple way back then, when men wore pants and the women mend,

Shirts and socks and dresses too.

Both were equaled in what they'd do.

Men worked hard to buy a place, for women to clean and tie a lace.

So the children they had would not fall.

Over unlaced shoes while running in the hall.

Men were kings and the women were queens. Both worked hard to make a team.

Yes life seemed simple way back when

Women were women and men were men.

But now that's gone the simple life. Women are men and men are wives.

You were born a girl and changed to a boy.

You started with dolls and ended with war toys.

That's sexist you say with a very sly grin. that boys have dolls and the dolls have

men.

So where's the sexist is all I ask.

I had nothing to do with controlling the past.

I don't mind nailing up a board. My husband makes slippers with leather cords.

He can cook and clean and make a great stew.

While I work up a sweat at the gym in the school..

So when people get tired of who's ahead of who, don't tell a soul lest they laugh at

you.

Because as long as women are women and men can jest.

Just be true to yourself and to heck with the rest.

LITTLE BUGGERS

Little buggers, little buggers, little buggers everywhere.

Little buggers in your clothing, little buggers in your hair.

Little buggers on the clothes line, little buggers on the lawn.

Little buggers flying in your mouth, when you go to take a yawn.

Always bugging, always landing, and flying round your face,

making lots of bugging noises everywhere and everyplace.

Little buggers always bugging when you want to swim or play.

Little buggers are mosquitoes on a hot and humid day.

YOU CAN'T

You can't see the forest because of the trees.

You can't collect honey because of the bees.

You can't do all this because of all that.

You can't lose your weight because you're too fat.

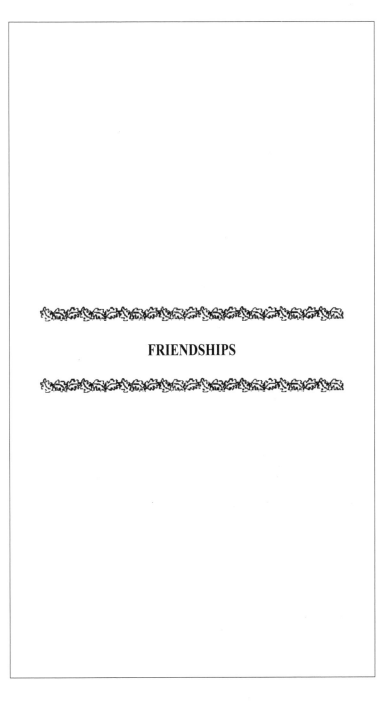

FRIENDSHIPS

CONNIE

She was a student, she never cursed.
She just wanted to be a psychiatric nurse.

We became friends, ole Connie and me.
She was so wild, so single, and free.

We laughed a lot and told lots of jokes.
Sometimes she'd give me a couple of pokes.

Connie made friends wherever she went.
Time with our Connie is always well spent.

It was one of these times we were dining on soup.
When she looked at me funny and called me "Old turkey poop".

Ever since then we made it our pack,
to call each other "Ole turkey poop" back.

I met Connie's family who then numbered three.
There was Fred, Anne-the author, and sister, Peg-gie.

I heard of her children, Deanne and Nile too.
Connie was one of the best friends that I knew.

We went separate ways ole Connie and me.
but we never lost touch with each other, no Sir-ee.

She had lots a fellers, I know this is true.
Cause I met and wished I could have kicked quite a few.

But finally she told me of Erkki's kind ways.
Doubtfully I said, "Best beware at your age.

She assured me he was kind and generous too.
Well the first time I met him I knew it was true.

I can see massages for Erkki and such,
She'll sure pick his brain too without much of a fuss.

She came to see me and tried to pick mine.
But I sure fooled her cause there was none to be find.

Ed, he just laughed and said with a grin.
"Connie, you know Judy and where it has been?"

Now the four of us are friendly and get along fine.
We'll even visit one another time after time.

Erkki's a great host who's witty and quick.
I've met his two sons, They are Kari and Nick.

They're here for the wedding and then they'll go home.
But Connie now married will never more roam.

No matter, with Connie we'll have lots of fun.
Now Erkki and Ed can get the things done.

And, as long as they don't holler or gripe.
We wives will promise, not to punch out their lights.

My poetry has ended. There's nothing more to say,
except to my friends "May God bless you today."

YOU ARE SUCH A SPECIAL FRIEND

You are such a special friend.
You always come to mind.
When I'm sad and missing you.
It takes me back to old times.
When we would play and giggle
At the silly things boys would say.
Remember when they noticed our boobs
We'd shy and run away.

Remember, too, that stupid time?
When I did that dumb joke?
I pulled the chair away from you
And your back you broke, almost.
I never meant to hurt you friend.
It was the stupid way I was.
I never did that joke again
Cause I love you just because.

So here's my promise to you my friend
If you ever need some cheer.
Just call on me when you're feeling low.
You'll know I'll always be near.

Donna & Bill
50 Anniversary
1946 – 1996

Donna, you were beautiful, and Bill you were handsome too.
I'm so proud that you asked of me to do this poem for you.

But a poet I'm not, a poet per say…
yet I'm here to share special memories today.

So let's start the story and how it begun…
Donna had met Bill while skating for fun.

Roller skating then was a popular sport.
So it seemed very natural for Billy to court.

Now Bill is a guy who doesn't waste time
as he said to his Donna, "Will you be mine?"

And Donna whose head is always on straight,
looked at her Billy said "Oh, I can't wait."

So two hearts were bonded on that special night,
and six months later they became Man & Wife.

They wed in September, the weather rather cool.
Bill in his last year at Franklin High School.

They both settled down to married life as such

The money was scarce and the burdens were much.

It wasn't always easy for Donna and Bill.

The days making money seemed all the way uphill.

Then dentistry called Bill and the feeling it grew.

He had to leave town, a career to pursue.

He left Donna behind, But what could he do?

He came home once a month for a year, no….. two.

Bill's parents lived close, a blessing I'm sure.

the family had grown. they now numbered four.

B. J. was the first one to enter this world.

she was cute and was cuddly, and oh what a girl!

The grandparents loved her as she tried to break loose.

They couldn't get enough of their little papoose.

And Vince was the second and also the last.

They loved him too he was such a blast.

Think nick-named him Porky and I don't know why.

But he was their precious and the apple of their eye.

If now they could see him with Sarah by his side.

Their hearts would be so happy filled with family pride.

The same pride felt by Donna for her Shayme and Shayne.

And Bill's so proud of his family that he'd do it all over again.

And raising a family is no easy task.

One must have hobbies to help the time pass.

For Bill it was climbing and mountains to tame,

from Columbia to Ecuador and back home again.

While Donna at home and her hobbies to do.

She'd refinish wood and varnish it too.

The week-ends were fun, water skiing at "The Bow",

with friends Rodney and Mary and all the gear in tow.

But now they live quiet, a life more at ease

at their cabin near Whitefish with big tall, tall trees.

This is not over now and it doesn't end here.

There are friends and family who wish them good cheer.

If Anniversaries could fit the people they are for,

then yours should be so happy you couldn't ask for more.

I thank you for letting me write this in rhyme.

I'll do it again for your 70th next time.

So that's why this gathering is so very right,

all because of the bonding on that very special night.

FIFTY YEARS OF FRIENDSHIP

Fifty years of friendship, fifty years or more.

I often think of the visits when I'd come to your kitchen door.

Time has changed us physically. We've grown older mentally too.

But with this new technology, why can't I e-mail myself to you?

Just think of all the fun we'd have, visiting, chatting, and sipping tea.

You'd have your mug and I'd have my china cup and we'd visit until three.

Then back I'd come via e-mail. I'd still have plenty of time:

to make the beds, get supper on, still clean up and shine.

You could e-mail yourself to my place. You could do it the very next day.

I'd take you to see lots of sights before you hurried away.

That way I wouldn't miss you so much, like now when I sometimes do.

Thinking back over these fifty years. What would I do without you?

God must have known what I needed, a friend through thick and thin.

I'm so thankful for our rare friendship made possible only through Him.

So may God bless and keep you, safe from any unseen harm.

I thank you for the memories made when we were down on the farm.

A friendship like ours is special. A friendship like ours is rare.

I composed this poem for you my friend to show how much I care.

Roger

There's a light at Bridge City

That will no longer shine.

He was a friend to all.

And to all he was kind.

The smile on his face

when he greeted you " Good Day"

showed you somehow

he cared in a personal way.

He was tactful and honest

And respected you too.

There was no minor service

That he wouldn't do.

You were his business

But also his Friend.

We will miss you dear Roger

May your memory never end..

Betty and Otto's

50th Anniversary

1952 - 2002

Betty and Otto lived a long life.
50 years of marriage as husband and wife.

Many friends and family too are gathered here today.
To wish you love and happiness as you journey on your way.

But let's go back and see how far since it all began.
When Betty was a pesky girl and Otto a shy young man.

Yes, Betty was quite the girl and quite the little pest.
Otto tried to avoid her, he tried his very best.

But Betty would have none of it and teased him just the same.
If Eddie didn't rescue him he'd call her a nasty name.

But Betty was persistent and quite the stubborn girl.
She blossomed out quite nicely setting Otto's heart a twirl.

Her mother said to Otto, "You stop being such a mouse.
It's time to marry Betty if you're going to play house."

So married they got by a man named McLean.
Who tied the knot tight so they'd always remain...

married for life like some birds of the air.
You know the ones... they travel in pairs.

How proud he would be for the knot he done tied.
Fifty years married this husband and bride.

Then off to Saskatchewan both of them went.
They lived in a house with very high rent.

They rented that house two sizes too small .
They had only two rooms with four to eight walls.

Then they had enough they decided to move
to a rent free garage with no swimming pool.

Then they lived in the bush surrounded by trees.
A chipmunk would visit getting almonds for free.

The children they came to Otto's greet glee.
Five little sprouts to the Herman Family tree.

There was Darryl and Brenda and Randy made more.
Then Barry and Merlin but who's keeping score?

In summer Otto worked. the soil he did plow.
Many nights he worked late by the sweat of his brow.

The cows calved, dogs barked and the birdies did sing.
They didn't have enough money to buy a shoe string.

But each other they had to lean on and depend.
Their belief in God saw many troubles end.

Ten summers they spent down South near the sea.
A place far from home, a place called Belize.

They helped build a hospital and helping the poor.
They delivered babies and did so much more.

Now they just stay home with their hobbies each one.
One is for profit and one is for fun.

Otto, he, sits watching 3ABN
problem solving the woes of his good fellowmen.

But sometimes his hobby gets him in deep.
You see Otto's retired and his hobby is <u>SLEEP</u>

And Betty does baking. The best stuff around.
She attends Farmer's Markets, out here and in Town.

But now they're retired and living alone.
The kids have all gone to make homes of their own.

So this is the story of my two very best friends.
I'd like to go on, but I know I must end.

Yes this is the end and I hope it was fine.
I'll do it again if you just say the time.

But now as I close I'd just like to say.
I wish for you Love on your Special Day.

"And when Heaven pull the curtains back and pins it with a star.
Don't forget that we'll love you no matter where you are."

Elaine Roque

I know of a woman who's really okay.
She's a very grand woman named Elaine Roque.
She has many talents and her faults are so few.
She cares allot about others...
I wish I did. Don't you ?

Her husband supports her with a love so very grand.
With him right beside her, on the Solid Rock they stand.
Her children are her first love, but they won't be her last.
Her other love is vespers.
At her house, it's a blast !

God has blessed her with helping out others.
Taking in and looking after those without mothers.
It's a blessing God gave her right from above.
And she'll do it faithfully,
cause its God's plan she loves.

If I were given one friend to save my life.
Elden I'd choose, Elaine, your dear wife.
For I know she'd save me with the father above.
She'd welcome me here, with arms opened in love.

To Elaine, my dear friend, what more can I say?
except that I admire you in most every other way.
You seem to have energy with so much to spare.
I know you must get tired with the burdens that you bare.

But you're a good example of what Christ-like should be.
May God continue to bless you on your 50th Birthday
AND throughout eternity.

DOWN MEMORY LANE

Miss. McLeod

Her hair was so lovely of that I can recall,
when she walked the isle ways of the one room school hall.
She taught like a Pro at only eighteen.
She was our first teacher and she was our queen.
We all loved her dearly.
she stayed only two years.
And oh how we missed her
and cried many a tears.

She married a farmer when she moved away.
It was many years later before a glad Reunion day.
We kept faithfully in touch until the letters they ceased.
She didn't respond and she couldn't be reached.
Her son sent the news,
she was now laid to rest.
The world lost a Teacher
she was one of the best.

HAPPY FATHER'S DAY

My head upon your chest I place.
Your gentle breath sweeps across my face.
Your arms around me safe and sound,
protecting me from unseen harm.

Feeling secure and safe at ease.
Loving you so it pleases me.
My Lover, Protector, Husband, and Friend
putting up with my insecurities until the end.

You're trusting and brave. A man without guile.
You're always there to help me smile.
Father's Days may come and may go.
but I don't need a special day to love you so.

I write poems about those I love,
like friends and family and God above.
I write poems about the deep blue sea.
But here is one for you from me.

Remember, you are my hero, you are also my life.
I thank you and love you and glad I'm your wife.

OUR LIFE

Our era's almost over. It's soon time to say good-bye.
A generation has since blossomed out since our parents died.

We, too, must take that final trip into the bleak unknown.
And rest our shells that once held us when we were flesh and bone

Memories of us, too, will fade. as our thoughts become old too.
The only memory we will leave here, will be "the burden of our existence" You.

Because if it wasn't for us. You wouldn't have come to be.
So we had a part of all of this, from the bud to the family tree.

SUTHERLAND'S RIVER WALK

Just walk around the River
Just for old time's sake.
Just a walk around the River,
before it is too late.

We'll walk the River slowly,
remembering days gone by,
when you and I were younger
and the geese were flying high.

The Autumn leaves were falling
gently down around the ground,
in rainbow brightly colors of
yellows, reds, and browns.

We'll pass the one room school house
and on up the Thorburn Road.
We might even see some "Meeses",
or even some baby toads.

We'll pass the neighbor's houses.
A few of them we know.
They'll wave to us as we pass by,
and we'll wave back a fond hello.

We'll dream of the days of swimming,
down by the River's bank
when your father came and saved me.
I owed him many a thanks.

Halloween nights were the fun times.
We'd excite ole " Teddy" the pup.
But I was the one so excited.
So excited that I'd throw up.

I had a lot of sleep-overs,
and lots of food so keen.
It'd be hard to find a mom who'd cook
as good as Mama Jean.

But now we're married with kids of our own,
and all we can do is dream.
The world has changed since we were young.
Nothing is as good as it seems.

So when we meet again for one last time.
Please,… for this favor I plea.
Just take your hand and place it in mine,
and walk round the River with me.

VETERANS

Some look at you and start to laugh

Some look at you and say.

"Why do we care for these old folks

and of those who passed away?

But let me set you straight my friend

And let me tell you plain.

If it wasn't for those ones you laugh at

Your freedom would be in vain.

So instead of swearing and not giving a care

Take another look and see.

Those dear ole souls who fought for us

So that your freedom would be free.

Free to say things you do

about the way you feel

Free to do what you do now

By calling them a heel

But someday soon and old you'll be

And someone to you will laugh.

At the way you walk, and the way you talk

You'll feel hurt about that.

So start anew and change your tune

About the way you act today.

Be humble enough to say well done

If they should limp your way.

GONE

Gone are the hugs and kisses galore. Gone are the overnight stays.
Gone from my breast, but not from my heart.
Gone are the happier days.

Gone are the fun times while sleeping over. Gone are memories we'll make.
Gone from my breast, but not from my heart.
Glad is: I'm happy for your sake.

Here stays the heartache that beats within me. Here stays the tears that I weep.
Here stays the pillow stained with my love.
Here stays the memories I'll keep.

Come to my breast my little love. Come to my heart and stay.
You may be gone far away from me now.
But my memories will not fade away.

MEMORIES OF YOU

Looking at your pictures many words are left untold.
Realizing you're but a memory now.
Never to grow old.

Memories come of times before.
The day we said Good-bye.
Some were happy some were sad.
The question is still, why?

Why was it that you left us here?
Instead of the other way?
Grandparents are to outlive their kids?
NO! They're supposed to lead the way

But here we sit among the memories
And frames of shining gold,
Looking at your pictures,
Many words are left untold.

MISS   M.

Oh how we first loved you,
when we stared at your sweet face.

The day you came into our world
filled us with awe and grace.

The more we got to know you,
the more bonded we became.

But things did happen to make us sad
and they were never the same.

We missed you for the longest time.
We cried for you most nights.

But someday if we'd be patient and kind,
things would turn out all right.

And sure enough it happened.
In fact the day before Xmas Eve.

Grampa talked it over with your Mom
and bless her, she agreed.

77

We always waited and hoped for the best.

And so somehow we knew.

That letting your mother trust us again,

we just knew we'd get to see you.

We can't speak for your bio father,

that's something only he can do.

But all we can tell you is this my dear,

we most certainly do love you.

Even tho the time was long

before you came back to us

The main thing now is to love you

forever without a whole lot of fuss.

So no matter where you go my dear

and no matter what you do,

Grampa and I will always be here

to assist your mother and you.

A GOOD NAME

I don't want to be famous
I don't want to be known.
I just want to write poems
Before I head toward home.

I just want to leave something
For my grandkids to find.
So I'll leave them my poems
From the thoughts in my mind.

Life is so funny.
We are born and we die.
We await resurrection
In the ground neath the sky.

So when my time comes
And I'm on my way.
" We'll miss you dear Nana."
I hope my grandkids will say.

Because you can have lots of money
And be noted for your fame.
But if your family don't love you.
What good is your name?

OCEAN MEMORY

I didn't realized how much I missed it.
I didn't realize how much I cared.
The site, the sound, the smell of it
The gentle salt mist on my hair

Yesterday I did recapture it
Boxed in a place so right.
Today I'll reinforce it
In my memories of tonight.

The sight of it is so majestic
The sounds and smell are too.
I can hear the gentle lapping
Feel it lapping against my shoe.

I feel the mist upon my lids.
Hear the gulls call to the waves.
Feel the drawing of my body
Like a magnet, to the caves.

Caves where the ocean rushes inward
Spewing out great gulps of sea
When the incoming meets the outward
No place to go but to retreat.

Beautiful Ocean, so majestic
So relaxing but only deceives.
Yet you are so very brutal
And destructive as you can be

Waves as high as ten stories
So strong they can pound you dead.
You can't tame the mighty ocean.
Even Moby and that's his bed.

I love you mighty ocean and
I respect your deceiving waves.
I learned my lesson as a child
When nearly met a watery grave.

Yes, I hear you when you call me.
Beaconing me to the deep blue sea.
Perhaps someday I WILL surrender
Then you'll have whats left of me.

But for now I choose to love you.
And everything that you stand for.
I will hide you in my memory
Till I wish to unlock the door.

YOU CAN'T GO BACK

You can't go back of that I know.

Don't let some people tell you so.

I have tried and I have found,

myself on unfamiliar ground.

But though I knew what was to be,

you can never go back to memories.

Your past is something only left

to those who wish to take a guess.

You may think that this is a slap.

But I know what I'm getting at.

Trust me now as I've been back

And being back was just so slack.

No longer are the good old days

They're gone for good " The good old ways".

So hear me out I would not lie.

But we've been back there both Ed and I.

We can't return to what was then.

People change as rainbows bend.

The best thing to do is forge ahead.

Past the bridges of strife, left unsaid.

I kid you not really I do

What once was kind and good for you,

is no longer to be found,

on Canada's ocean playing ground.

If you leave there just don't return.

Otherwise, count those bridges burned.

Too many changes must be endured

and wondering why the province is poor.

It's not the same as it was to me.

Why wasn't it like it used to be?

I loved the place where I was born.

But to live there now is so forlorn.

So, Go back West! is what I say

Go visit back East another day.

The Ocean Playground is no longer home.

You belong out West where the cowboys roam.

Don't leave the West my heart did say

When we moved east that fateful summer day.

We got to the border then the car broke down.

It was then that we should have turned round.

But no not I, it's the East for we

What can the Prairies now hold for me?

Wake up, wake up you foolish girl.

Don't you know your leaving a pearl?

The West is weeping. The rain is raw.

You will return at next spring's thaw.

Oh Ed, Oh Jude, why do you go?

We love you here where the Chinook wind blows.

We'll morn your passing till your return.

From Nova Scotia let your bridges be burned.

The sea can't hold you like, once, it did.

The flat, wild prairies put in their bid.

You must decide finally where it will be.

Will you make your home the West or is it the sea?

Will I be a traitor if I claim West once more?

But how can I abandon my walking on the shore?

I love the West, but also the sea.

I guess the final decision rests souly on me.

A MOMENT IN TIME

A moment in time is a theme of mine to think back of the days gone by.

When whispered the trees to the ears of the bees,

And the days were sunny and sublime.

We'd swim in the pool to keep ourselves cool and drink from the pump at the well.

The days were long with the winter now gone

And in silence sits the ole school bell.

Ah, the days of youth, how fast they flee with never a speed bump around.

Yesterday we are babies in our mother's arms.

Tomorrow we are graduation bound.

What lies ahead we do not know, nor can we find out why.

To see some go and live full lives,

While others, less fortunate, die.

But to carry on in the same ole way is not to advance at all.

So make up your mind, to your past be kind.

To the future.... give it your all.

SEVEN HOURS APART

I want to write a poem
about Kirsten Robyn Knox.
She lives in St. Paul
and presents me with rocks.

She spoils me rotten.
She's always in my heart.
I don't see her often,
cause we're seven hours apart.

But, when we're together
we have lots of fun.
She paints me with make up
and makes my eyes run.

My cheeks get all rosy.
I look like I am flushed.
But she makes me look that cozy
by piling on the blush.

THE TEDDY BEAR

You looked so sad and lonely lying there in the bin.
You were so ragged and dirty and your ribbon was worn so thin.

I picked you up to check you. I looked from front to back.
All you seemed in need of was a good hot soapy bath.

To me you were a sweetheart, furry, and soft, and brown.
I tried to throw you back again but I couldn't put you down.

You needed someone to love you. Someone who wanted to keep......
A memory of her two dear pets whom. A week before were put to sleep.

I was the one who would love you. I will take you, with me, back West.
You will be loved in me memory of my cats who are now at rest.

Someday you will find another to love you until the end.
Because you are so cuddly, they too will become your friend.

You were once somebody's plaything. You were once somebody's toy.
But, like me, they discarded you. You no longer brought them joy.

It wasn't your fault you're discarded. It wasn't your fault you cried.
To have your love rejected...... hurts something awful inside.

You ended up in the bin unwanted until the day that I passed by.
And saw in you something worthy. Something no one could deny.

That something is a longing. A longing to someone belong.
A longing that on one will understand, when all things you do are wrong.

But like me you have a someone. Someone who'll love you so strong.
You'll never have to worry now, for to me you'll always belong.

FAMILY TIMES

I shall remember the good times that we shared,
as families so rarely do.
Of fishing, swimming, and picnicking.
They're just to name a few.

Family Days were happy then
when families kept in touch.
We'd play and sing and fooled around
with those we loved so much.

Problems were few and far between.
But we had them just the same.
To get along with each his own
was a feat to not cast any blame.

GOOD OLE DAYS

Whatever happened to the "Good Ole Days?"
The days when we were young.
We clowned around and did some stunts
But, we'd never hurt no one.

Something happened to make us change.
To be the type of people we are.
You went your way and I went mine.
Both following a different star.

Our sense of humor is all but gone.
In an adult world we live now.
Why can't we see the funny things?
Have we've grown up too fast somehow?

Someday the answers may return.
And rid us of our fears.
Of not staying youthful while growing up.
But we continue on through the years.

What will become of you and I
until we are laid to rest?
Will you go your way and I'll go mine?
Or else meet in "The Land of the Blest?"

Time will come and time will go
and life will continue on.
But for you and I and our youthful days,
our memories will linger on.

THROUGH THE YEARS

Through the years we've had our many sorrows.
Through the years we've shed so many tears.
Through the years we never thought about tomorrows.
Just remaining together through the years.

Through the years we've seen a lot of good times.
Through the years we faced uncertain fears.
Through the years we've done it all together.
And that remains important through the years.

Through the years we depended on each other.
Through the years we've had differences to bear.
Through the years we've argued then and often.
But we've forgotten why through the years.

Through the years my mind recalls the romance.
Through the years the memories we hold dear.
Through the years my mind keeps on recalling.
How you stood by me faithfully through the years.

MEMORIES OF MY DAD

Henry Willie Pettipas
NOV. 7, 1904 – DEC. 19, 1965
born in D'Escousse, Cape Breton to William Pettipas & Rebecca Bonin

TRIBUTES TO MY DAD

I remember the time by the Oceanside
with lumber you built a boat.

It was the maiden voyage and
you guaranteed that it would float.

We got into the middle or
what it seemed to me,

was not the river I thought it was
but the middle of the deep blue sea.

The boat, it took on some water.
I was sure that we would drown.

but calmly you just canned it out,
I felt safe when you were around.

You were mostly there when I needed you.
I wish I could say the same.

I was so young and foolish then
of many things I was ashamed.

I wish I had told you
that I loved you so very much,

instead of wishing you here right now.
for your hands I'd love to touch.

But memories of the happier times
sustain me through these years,

and memories of my precious Dad,
I can view them through my tears.

MY DADDY

Awesome memories of you come flooding down
Through the memory lane of my mind.
Sitting beside the ocean, you
beside me, I can find.

Remembering all the good times,
of the days gone by before.
The ocean sounds, and
sites and smells
bring your presence to my door.

The times when you would take me out
and with your steady hands.
Show me ways to find the shells
and the hiding places of the clams.

Together, we would dig for them,
and slowly fill the pot.
Then, the fire we would build
to cook… and eat them while they're hot.

Only the oysters we'd eat raw.
I can feel them sliding down.
But now my taste lies in other things.
Since you're no longer around.

TEARS OF YESTERDAY

Tears of yesterdays flow gently down
and round my face and cheek.
I have my memories and lots of them.
When I need... I take a peek.
But certain things just trigger it,
like the waves that lap at shores.
The squawk of the gulls gliding up high.
The salty smell of the sea, that, and so much more.

Memories are all that's left
of what I have of you.
That and some old pictures which..
I'd say number about.. maybe two.
The ocean smells aren't the only things
that triggers the memories I have.
I also have the smell of your cologne
To comfort me when I'm sad.

ABANDONED (AGAIN)

Dec. 19, 1965 you left me

behind….

You also left behind:

your jacket and contents:

a small bottle of
Bayer's Aspirins.

one quarter, 2 pennies.

a small box
of Eddy (wooden) matches.

& your overalls

which was once white canvas,

now gray with hard, cracked, dry, paint.

of

various colors.

and …

Your Cologne:

Old Spice

A boxed set of

white sails

on a red background.

Used

after a hard day of

climbing ladders, painting objects

in the hot sun.

Coming home, washing up,

and

shaving a shadow
of

advancing whiskers.

While looking into a

cracked,

five by seven,

mirror,

hanging by

a triangle

of

white string

on the kitchen window.

Afterwards

slapping

both cheeks

with the palms of your hands.

Then

noticing

the face

of the young child

you left behind,

gazing

in awe

at your daily ritual:

Me.

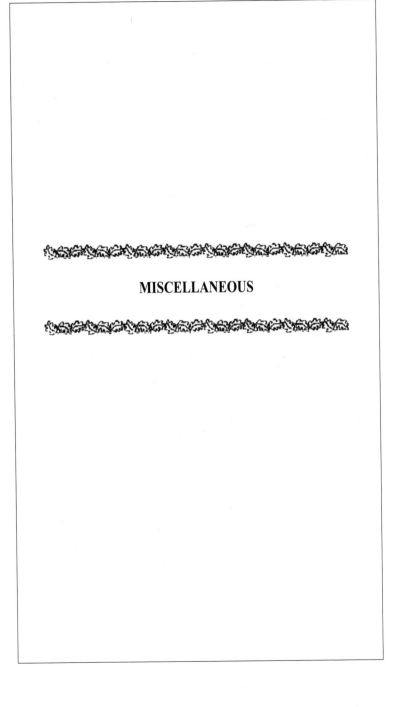

MISCELLANEOUS

BECAUSE OF DAD

There is an open family Bible
On the desk by the tree.
Where father would daily read it
To my brother and to me.

Many nights of weeping
We'd hear him by the bed.
Crying for our souls to save
Since mother's long since dead.

He would do the proper things
To bring us up just right.
To own up to our own mistakes
Not to cower or take flight.

But that took place so long ago.
It hardly seems worthwhile.
To see how successful we've become
Since we were both a child.

My brother is a Doctor.
And I am one to boot.
We thank our father long since gone.
For giving us strong roots.

DRUNKARD

You're a drunken bum they once told me. You'll not amount to a thing.
I may be a drunken bum to you my friend. But in the eyes of my daughter I'm a
king.

She loves me when I stagger and fall. She loves me when I swear.
She even loves me when I sell her gifts...... to buy more beer.

I took her once to a movie show. Her school friends she saw near.
I fell into the gutter drunk. She helped me up from there.

Was she ashamed? A little I think. But how could I be sure?
She never said she hated me. She only loved me more.

If I had the chance to live again. And prove to her my love.
I'd probably do the same darn thing. Because that's what drinking does.

Pougies, I never said I loved you I never said I cared.
I tried to show you by my ways and sometimes even be there.

So don't go thinking I didn't care or that I didn't give a dang.
I loved you so my little mousie even tho I was a bum of a man.

MOTHER TERESA
1910 – 1997

Her talent was a gift from God.
He planted within her heart.
She used that talent to care for the poor,
Too sick to do their part.

She never wanted wealth or fame
Or popularity by the score.
She only wanted to ease the pain
Of the homeless and the poor.

Now that she's gone her light has gone out.
Or so some people say
But Mother T. will always be
Shining in the poor always.

THOUGHTS OF YOU

Here I sit as I oft times do
Thinking and dreaming thoughts of you.
Of the way things were long ago.
When you and I would always know
How each one felt by emotions we'd show.

It seems so long since you left me.
I continue on although I see.
I'd rather have you here to complete my life.
Instead I face the future as your widowed wife.

It's the little things that remind me of you.
The chair where you sat.
The book almost new.
The shaving gear idle beside the sink.
The empty glass from which you'd drink.

The good old days of "Travel the world."
The horses we rode.
The rope that we twirled.
Everything now is in the past tense.
There's nothing left for me ever since
you went.

OLD FOLKS

We keep alive our memories of days of way back when.
To help us trough our golden years when sad times oft sets in.

So many years have come and gone of the days when we were spry.
But now we only sit and think. Our strength has long passed by.

Some folks who live in old folks homes have long since given in
.and resigned themselves to live out life for to continue would be sin.

Their youth has long sense passed them by. They are unable to do what they could.
They are lonely and deserted now. They feel their worth is no good.

They used to love and go on dates in the days of yesteryear.
It's by a lonely window they sit now unnoticed.... With a dry stained tear.

Since sin came in life is gone of that we are guaranteed
So here we stand watch and wait for visits from you or me.

Here today and gone tomorrow, such a quote it seems unfair.
So love them now while they're around. Cause tomorrow they may not be there.

They're mothers, fathers, and grandparents too. They're sick and know not where,
They've been or gone or going to. They just wait for death in their chair

How often do we pass them by in the hospitals or on the street?
We see their struggle with their life, but them we wouldn't want to meet.

So please be careful when you speak to them….. not harshly or cold.
Cause years from now you will be greeted the same when your weak and old.

ANNE

She sang like an angel. Her hair like spun gold.

Her voice was sweet and mellow as her story she'd unfold.

She'd sing about her Jesus and His love to her He gave.

Death cannot deny her, for her He died to save.

She's sleeping now and waiting. No pain to her belongs.

So till we see her once again, We'll miss her stories in sweet song.

RIDE THE RIVER

If you rode the river and I was by your side,

And if you roped me tightly I'd be happy as your bride.

Side by side we'd ride together down life's very twisting road

Maybe once we'd ride on separate.. no!...Together we'll share the load.

BLAME

I blamed you for allot of things that happened in my life.
I blamed you for the hurt I felt when abandon by my wife.

I blamed you for this spot I'm in not knowing right from wrong.
Even the lie of child abuse, to you that also belonged.

I've had so many ups and downs at times I wasn't sure.
Whether I'd be loved again…..less, the same, or more.

If you could put your hand in mine and relive the miles with me
Would you not think that I deserve to be the son you see?

Special Enclosure

My friend, of fifty plus years, wrote a story for me. I have included it in this book because it has a special meaning for me and we have a friendship that has spanned over five decades. A milestone that not too many can lay claim to in this day and age. The following story is her own words and was sent to me, which I would like to share with you.

The Clovers

Once upon a time, there was a little girl named Joyce. She lived in a far away place called Hammonds Plains. She was a very busy little girl as she had to weed the garden and feed the hens and wash the dishes and much, much, more. On July 4th, 2001 she was kind of tired of working, and also a bit lonely. She missed her friend Judy-Ann who lived far, far away.
She missed the farm where they once played together. She missed the "Meeses "by the River. She missed the singing songs together with her friend Judy-Ann. She missed going to the "Little Red School House", and she missed their favorite teacher "Kay". She thought about the day Judy-Ann shared her new bicycle and even let the little girl named Joyce learn to ride it. Joyce was lonely cause she missed the fields where she used to pick strawberries."

She missed the River where they used to swim together.
About 3 O clock Joyce said to herself. I am quitting my work. I am going to get the mail. So she did. And guess what was in the mailbox? – 2 letters from her friend Judy-Ann. They had nice cards inside and even a wonderfully true, beautiful poem. (Fifty Years of Friendship) Joyce was so happy that some tears came to her eyes. She was so happy that she went off picking strawberries-something that she loved to do. While picking, she saw a cluster of clover. She thought about finding a 4-leaf clover for her friend Judy-Ann, to send to her far, far away. She no sooner started looking when she found not 1, but 2 lovely 4 leaf clovers. She couldn`t believe her eyes. She kept looking-but there were no more. Just 2-no more, no less. She thanked God for helping her to find them: - One for Judy-Ann and one for her pal-Eddy. A funny feeling came over her. "How come I only find 4 leaf clovers when I really need them? What a mystery ? What do You suppose is the answer? "
No matter what, These clovers mean good luck and she was very eager to send them off to her true friend Judy-Ann, the very next day.-And that is exactly what she did. To prove it, here are the 2 4 – leaf Clovers
     1 for Judy and
     1 for whomever she chooses to give it to.

THE END

P.S. This story is 100% true.